# ODD JOBS

By Virginia Loh-Hagan

Disclaimer: This series focuses on the strangest of the strange. Have fun reading about strange people and things! But please do not try any of these antics. Be safe and smart!

45th Parallel Press

Published in the United States of America by Cherry Lake Publishing
Ann Arbor, Michigan
www.cherrylakepublishing.com

Reading Adviser: Marla Conn MS, Ed., Literacy specialist, Read-Ability, Inc.
Book Designer: Melinda Millward

Photo Credits: © branislavpudar / Shutterstock.com, cover; © Groomee / iStock.com, 1; © Jacob Lund / Shutterstock.com, 5; © terra24 / iStock.com, 6; © cristianl / iStock.com, 7; © Eviled / Shutterstock.com, 8; © sirtravelalot / Shutterstock.com, 9; © Hadrian / Shutterstock.com, 10; © Nagel Photography / Shutterstock.com, 12; © PHOTO CREDIT PENDING, 13; © pixelliebe / Shutterstock.com, 14; © MagMos / iStock.com, 15; © FabrikaSimf / Shutterstock.com, 16; © melnikof / Shutterstock.com, 17; © thieury / Shutterstock.com, 18; © branislavpudar / Shutterstock.com, 19; © Alffoto / Dreamstime.com, 20; © Philip Willcocks / Shutterstock.com, 22; © Julie Clopper / Shutterstock.com, 23; © wwing / iStock.com, 24; © Microgen / Shutterstock.com, 25; © Fer Gregory / Shutterstock.com, 26; © photka / Shutterstock.com, 27; © Hung Chung Chih / Shutterstock.com, 28, 29; © plavevski / Shutterstock.com, 30

**45th Parallel Press** is an imprint of Cherry Lake Publishing.

Library of Congress Cataloging-in-Publication Data

Names: Loh-Hagan, Virginia, author.
Title: Odd jobs / by Virginia Loh-Hagan.
Description: Ann Arbor : Cherry Lake Publishing, [2018] | Series: Stranger than fiction |
    Includes bibliographical references and index.
Identifiers: LCCN 2017035394| ISBN 9781534107595 (hardcover) | ISBN 9781534109575 (pdf) |
    ISBN 9781534108585 (pbk.) | ISBN 9781534120563 (hosted ebook)
Subjects: LCSH: Occupations–Juvenile literature. | Job descriptions–Juvenile literature.
Classification: LCC HF5382 .L639 2018 | DDC 331.702–dc23
LC record available at https://lccn.loc.gov/2017035394

Printed in the United States of America
Corporate Graphics

## About the Author

Dr. Virginia Loh-Hagan is an author, university professor, former classroom teacher, and curriculum designer. Her oddest job is writing books about odd jobs. She lives in San Diego with her very tall husband and very naughty dogs. To learn more about her, visit www.virginialoh.com.

# Table of Contents

# Introduction

People work to make money. They need money to live. Money buys food. It buys houses. It buys things.

There are all kinds of jobs. Some jobs take place during the day. Some jobs take place at night. Some jobs take place in an office. Some jobs take place outside.

Some people do really odd jobs. But there are strange jobs. And then there are really strange jobs. They're so strange that they're hard to believe. They sound like fiction. But these jobs are all true!

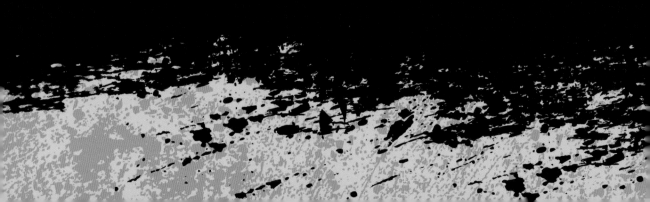

People train and study for their jobs.

# chapter one

# Vomit Cleaners

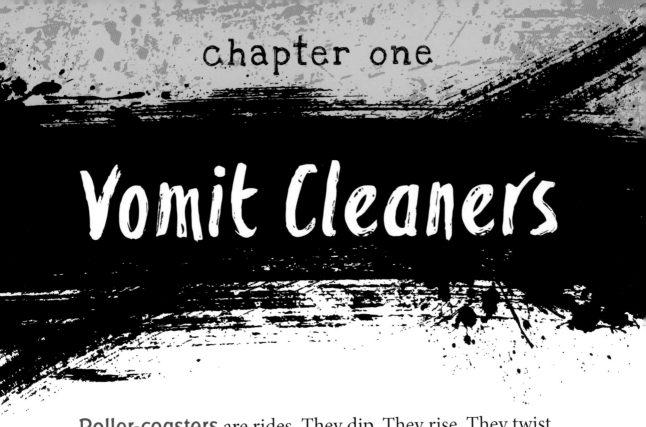

**Roller-coasters** are rides. They dip. They rise. They twist. They turn. Some people's stomachs can't take it. They **vomit**. Vomit means to throw up. This happens a lot on rides. The vomit smells bad. It looks bad. It has bad germs. It can make people sick. Some people may step in it. They might slip and fall.

Someone needs to clean the vomit. Vomit cleaners are a special type of **janitor**. Janitors are people who clean buildings. Vomit cleaners stand under scary rides. They wait for people to vomit. They show up with a mop and bucket. They clean it up. They keep parks safe.

*Amusement parks have rides and shows.*

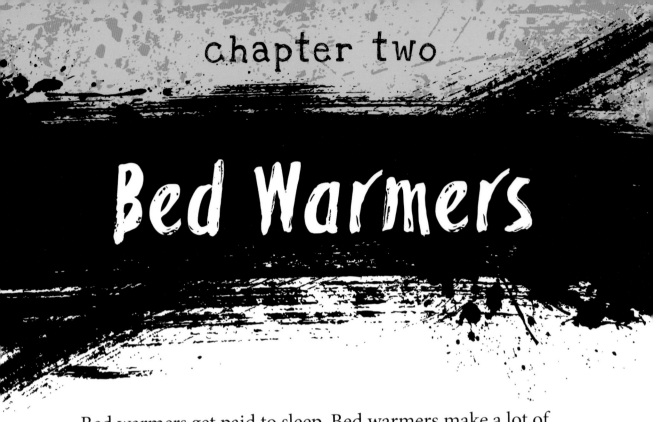

# chapter two

# Bed Warmers

Bed warmers get paid to sleep. Bed warmers make a lot of money. Some make over $200,000 per year. They sleep in hotel beds. They warm up beds. A hotel worker said it's like having a giant hot water bottle in your bed.

Guests stay in hotels. They come in from cold weather. They want a warm bed. Warm beds help people sleep better. Guests call for bed-warming service.

Bed warmers go to their rooms. They roll around in beds. They do this for 5 to 10 minutes. They do this before guests return to their rooms.

Bed warmers are like walking
electric blankets.

Bed warmers wear special suits. These suits cover them from head to toe. They're like a romper. They're made of wool. They keep people warm.

Bed warmers have a **thermometer**. Thermometers are tools. They measure cold. They measure heat. Bed warmers make sure beds are ready. They stay until beds are warm enough. They work until beds are perfect.

Professional sleepers have a similar job. They sleep in beds. They test beds. They help companies make better beds. They help people buy the best beds.

*Bed-warming jobs started in the United Kingdom.*

# Explained
# by Science

Workaholics are people who are addicted to work. They
work all the time. They ignore their family. They ignore
their friends. They don't take time to relax. They lose track
of time. Experts say it's not good to work all the time.
Workaholics have issues. They need to always be busy.
They may not think highly of themselves. They may have
stress. They may have problems getting along with people.
They don't work well in teams. They may not sleep enough.
They may have poor health. Experts think workaholism
runs in the family. It's passed down from parent to child.

# chapter three

# Duck Masters

Hyatt Regency Peabody is a hotel in Orlando, Florida. It has an odd job. It hires duck masters. The hotel has five ducks.

Duck masters walk the ducks. They do this twice a day. They start at 11:00 a.m. They get the ducks. The ducks live at the "Duck Palace." This is on the roof. Duck masters take the ducks down the elevator. They lead the ducks through the lobby. They walk on a red carpet. They talk to hotel guests. They talk about the ducks' lives. They show off the ducks. At 5:00 p.m., they walk the ducks again. They bring them back up to the roof.

*Marching the ducks is a famous tradition. It began in 1932.*

# chapter four

# Lipstick Readers

Lipstick readers read lipstick marks. They make people wear red lipstick. They make people kiss "love cards." Love cards are white paper. Lipstick readers read the lipstick **imprint**. Imprints are like stamps. They're the marks left by lips.

Lipstick readers study the lines. They study the shapes. They read messages. They tell people about themselves. They tell people about their pasts. They tell people about their futures. They tell people about their relationships. They make **predictions** about their lives. Predictions are guesses.

*Lipstick readers earn about $30 per reading.*

Lipstick readers mostly work at parties. They also work at fairs. Lipstick reading is fun. It's different. It amuses people.

# chapter five

# Paper Towel Sniffers

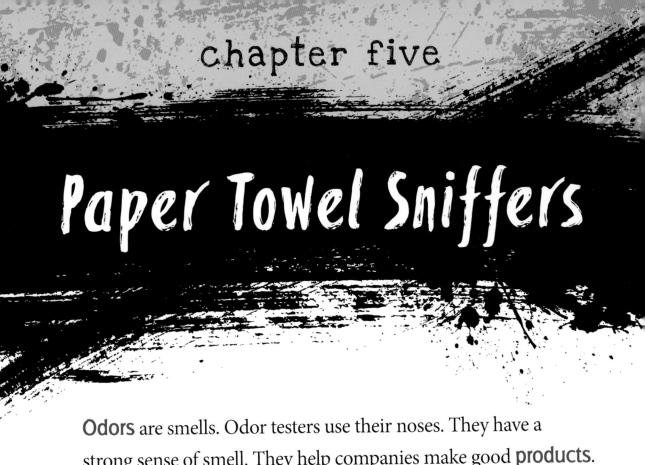

**Odors** are smells. Odor testers use their noses. They have a strong sense of smell. They help companies make good **products**. They help people buy good products. Products are things.

Most odor testers check for bad smells. They check for good smells. But paper towel sniffers check for no smells. Stinky paper towels don't sell well. Paper towel companies need paper towel sniffers. Paper towel sniffers are special odor testers. They test paper towels. They spend all day smelling paper towels. They make sure there's no smell.

They may have to travel. They make $1,000 per week.

Paper towels are made in giant rolls. Then they become the small rolls you use at home.

# chapter six

# Chicken Sexers

Thousands of chickens are born every day. Chicks are baby chickens. Female chickens are hens. They lay eggs. Male chickens are roosters. They're sold and eaten. Hens and roosters live different lives. They're treated differently. They get different food.

Chicken sexers sort day-old chicks. They separate males and females. This is not easy. Chicks all look the same. Chicken sexers need training. They need good eyes. They look at the shape of wings and feathers. They look at how long the wings and feathers are.

There's a special school to learn chicken sexing.

19

There's another way. They squeeze poop out of the chicks. They look for a bump on the chicks' bottoms. If there's a bump, it's a male. No bump means female. Chicken sexers need three years of training to learn how to do this.

Chicken sexers do the same thing over and over. They stand on their feet all day. They focus on one thing.

The best chicken sexers can sort 1,200 chickens per hour. They sort over a million chicks per year. They're highly **accurate**. Accurate means being correct. Chicken sexers make about $60,000 per year. They're hired by big chicken farms.

*There are chicken sexing contests.*

# Spotlight Biography

Manuel King was from the Texas-Mexico border. He grew up in the circus. He toured the United States and Mexico. King had an odd job. He was the world's youngest wild animal trainer. He began working with lions at age 7. On his 10th birthday, his father got him 10 lion cubs. He went into their cage. He played with them. He hugged them. He got lion-training lessons. His teacher was John "Chubby" Guilfoyle. Guilfoyle had one arm. He had an accident with a lion. King trained lions for over 30 years. He signed his letters with "Yours with a roar!" He died at age 92.

# chapter seven

# Human Statues

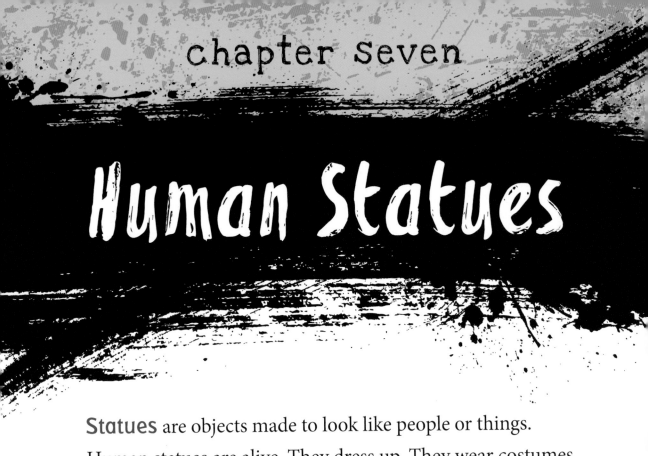

Statues are objects made to look like people or things. Human statues are alive. They dress up. They wear costumes. They wear makeup. They pose. They stand still. They stand for hours. They don't talk.

They're street artists. They find a popular spot. They wait for crowds. They stand still. Then, they make small moves. They do things like wink or wave. They surprise people. They work for **tips**. Tips are money. People give whatever they want. There's no set price.

There are contests. Many human statues participate.

Pretending to be statues was popular
at medieval and Renaissance parties.

23

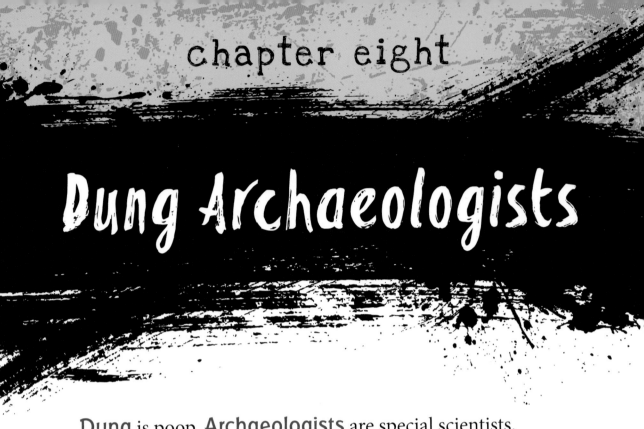

# chapter eight

# Dung Archaeologists

**Dung** is poop. **Archaeologists** are special scientists. They study things from the past. They study history. Many focus on **ancient** history. Ancient means from a very long time ago.

Dinosaurs pooped. Ancient humans pooped. Ancient animals pooped. Their poop turned into **fossils**. Fossils are remains that turned into rocks.

Dung archaeologists study old poop. They study shapes. They study sizes. They study how the fossils feel. They look for clues. They want to learn about ancient

*A dung archaeologist is called "Professor Poop" or "Doctor of Dung."*

times. They want to know how people lived. They want to know what they ate.

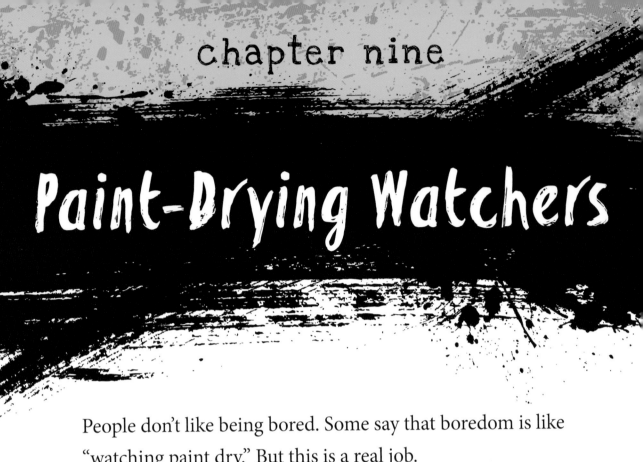

# chapter nine

# Paint-Drying Watchers

People don't like being bored. Some say that boredom is like "watching paint dry." But this is a real job.

Paint-drying watchers study paint. They put paint on cards. They put paint on walls. They watch the paint dry. They figure out how long it takes to dry. They time it. They touch paint. They test how sticky it is. They test paint in different weather. They see how tough the paint is. They see how the color changes. Wet paint looks different than dry paint.

Paint has a million tiny particles, or bits.

# chapter ten

# Panda Huggers

Pandas are bears. They have black-and-white fur. They have thick fur. They mainly live in China. They live in bamboo forests. They're protected. There are about 1,500 pandas in the wild. They need to grow in numbers. They're shy. They're independent. They don't have a lot of contact with humans.

The Conservation and Research Center for the Giant Panda is in China. It helps pandas. It hires panda huggers. It sent out a job notice. The notice said, "Your work has only one mission: Spending 365 days with the pandas and sharing in their joys and **sorrows**." Sorrow is sadness.

When born, baby pandas are the size of butter sticks.

Panda huggers have the best odd job. They're also called panda **nannies**. Nannies provide care. They usually watch small children.

Panda huggers take care of pandas all day. They hug pandas. They feed pandas. They clean pandas. They play with pandas. They get paid $32,000 per year. They get free meals. They get a free car. They get free housing. They need to be at least 22 years old. They should know about pandas. They should write well. They should know how to take pictures. They will share their experiences with the world. They will get others interested in pandas.

*Over 100,000 people applied to be a panda hugger. This crashed the Center's website.*

30

# Try This!

- Take a career test. Share things about what you like. Share your skills. These tests will tell you the type of jobs you could do.

- Go to a job fair. Learn about the different jobs out there.

- Create a resume. A resume lists your skills. It lists your training. It lists your references. References are people who can say good things about you.

- Ask to shadow someone at work. Follow this person around. Learn what this person does all day.

- Practice doing a job interview. Have a friend ask you questions. Answer the questions.

- Shop for nice work clothes.

# Consider This!

**Take a Position!** Learn about child labor laws. Labor means work. Do you think children should work? Argue your point with reasons and evidence.

**Say What?** 45th Parallel Press has a series of books called Odd Jobs. Read one of them. Summarize what you learned about the job. Explain what the job is. Explain how a person gets that job.

**Think About It!** What is your dream job? Create the job. Describe the job. What is the job title? What would you do? How would you spend your day?

## Learn More!

- Gerry, Lisa M. *100 Things to Be When You Grow Up*. Washington, DC: National Geographic Children's Books, 2017.
- Rosen, Michael J., and Ben Kassoy. *Weird Jobs*. Minneapolis, MN: Lerner Publishing Group, 2013.
- Weiss, Ellen. *Odd Jobs: The Wackiest Jobs You've Never Heard Of*. New York: Aladdin, 2012.

# Glossary

**accurate (AK-yuh-rit)** correct

**ancient (AYN-shuhnt)** from a long time ago, before modern times

**archaeologists (ahr-kee-AH-luh-jists)** scientists who study relics left behind by ancient civilizations

**chicks (CHIKS)** baby chickens

**dung (DUNG)** poop

**fossils (FAH-suhlz)** remains that have turned into rock over many years

**imprint (IM-print)** stamps, marks left behind as something is pressed

**janitor (JAN-ih-tur)** person who cleans buildings

**nannies (NAN-eez)** care providers, usually for young children

**odors (OH-durz)** smells

**predictions (prih-DIK-shuhnz)** guesses about the future

**products (PRAH-dukts)** things that people buy and sell

**roller-coasters (ROH-lur KOHST-urz)** amusement park rides that dip, rise, twist, and turn

**sorrows (SAHR-ohz)** things that cause sadness

**statues (STACH-ooz)** objects made to look like a person or thing

**thermometer (thur-MAH-mih-tur)** tool that measures the temperature of heat and cold

**tips (TIPS)** money people give away to others for performing a service

**vomit (VAH-mit)** to throw up

# Index